CROW-
WORK

Also by Eric Pankey

CROW-WORK

poems

Eric Pankey

MILKWEED EDITIONS

Published 2015 by Milkweed Editions
Printed in The United States of America
Cover design by Mary Austin Speaker
Cover photo by Kaz Tsuruta
Author photo by Rachel Eliza Griffiths
15 16 17 18 19   5 4 3 2 1
First Edition

Milkweed Editions, an independent nonprofit publisher, gratefully acknowledges
sustaining support from the Bush Foundation; the Jerome Foundation; the Lindquist &
Vennum Foundation; the McKnight Foundation; the National Endowment for the Arts;
the Target Foundation; and other generous contributions from foundations, corporations,
and individuals. Also, this activity is made possible by the voters of Minnesota through
a Minnesota State Arts Board Operating Support grant, thanks to a legislative
appropriation from the arts and cultural heritage fund, and a grant from the Wells Fargo
Foundation Minnesota. For a full listing of Milkweed Editions supporters, please visit
www.milkweed.org.

Library of Congress Cataloging-in-Publication Data

Pankey, Eric, 1959-
[Poems. Selections]
Crow-work : poems / Eric Pankey. -- First edition.
    pages cm.
ISBN 978-1-57131-454-3 (softcover : acid-free paper) -- ISBN 978-1-57131-884-8 (ebook)
I. Title.
PS3566.A575A6 2015
811'.54--dc23
                        2014031511

for Jennifer—again, always

Contents ::

CROW-
WORK

ASH

At the threshold of the divine, how to know
But indirectly, to hear the static as
Pattern, to hear the rough-edged white noise as song—

Wait, not as song—but to intuit the songbird
Within the thorn thicket, safe, hidden there.
Every moment is not a time for song

Or singing. Imagine a Buddha, handmade,
Four meters high of compacted ash, the ash
Remnants of joss sticks that incarnated prayer.

With each breath, the whole slowly disintegrates.
With each footfall, ash shifts. The Buddha crumbles.
To face it, we efface it with our presence.

An infant will often turn away as if
Not to see is the same as *not being seen*.
There was fire, but God was not the fire.

SPIRIT FIGURES

A few clouds like coils of incense ash.
Jay-squabble.
                    The day-moon on its owl perch.

A lanky fox noses at a dead hawk:
Startles, backs away, circles uncertain.

                    : :

That stalled moment in the trajectory
When an object neither rises nor falls

Is like seeing in your face the child you were:
Wholly you,
                    yet calm, unmarked by betrayals.

                    : :

The dead carry amber as torches,
Rub up static
                    a mirror fails to glean.

You are implied in the use of the *I*,
But only the *I* is complicit.

                    : :

Ragtag fog gathers like souls at river's edge.
Begin with chance and most anything's possible.

The woods, dark all day,
                        are bright with starlight—
Skirmish of embers in a dying fire.

: :

To hew a living flame, I let the pear
Dissolve into its own muddy sugars;

I mix powdered bone with seed,
                        toss it high,
And let each handful fall as a crow upon the snow.

: :

Once, you dragged a plank across an open grave,
That I might, if I chose,
                        traverse the gap and depth.

Now, you're lost in an atom's labyrinth.
How little I remember of time squandered.

: :

Empty hills.
             Clouds bank against evening.
Voices in the distance, but no one in sight.

A thousand autumn rains water the wilderness.
Voices in the distance, but no one in sight.

             : :

You are implied in the use of the *I*,
But only the *I* is complicit.

Alive with hunger, wired with fear, the fox,
Your envoy, said nothing.
                    I understood.

WHEN WE MEET ON THAT BEAUTIFUL SHORE

I keep speaking so as not to disappear.
The horizon:
            a long drag of charcoal.

A hawk banks,
            pivots on a wingtip, plunges.
How late the light endures then is gone.

There is no cause,
            only correspondence.
To animate the hitherto static

I place a word in front of the last.
Night:
            a long portage through a forest.

Pleasure no greater for its deferral.
The stone rests
            as water moves around it.

To enter Heaven, I must cross a wide river.

THE BOOK OF AN HOUR

How endless an hour seems compared to a proportionless forever.

In the realm of a poem only words are native.

Rain. Clouds like ravens' coats. A brawl of water over rocks.

The past is a book left out in the rain: ink blurs, pages fuse together.

Although the two deer are gone, their shadows hold on in the wet grass.

You know the story— a thread slips from a needle's eye.

WORKING IN THE DARK

In the flickering cave-light, a body is almost tangible.

An image coalesces, suspends upon a breath and is gone.

The mud is sluggish, cold.

By *image* we mean the visible vestiges of the invisible, we mean
that which cannot extricate itself from a gaze: these spectral
silhouettes, for instance.

To see the past we seclude ourselves in cave-depth.

To see the past we descend.

Are those two horses?

Or is that a horse outflanked by its shadow?

CROW-WORK

The in-held breath is released. Overhead, crows
(What will later be a field of gleaning crows)
Swoop and veer, an illegible cursive script.

There must be an equation for defining
The long odds that Vesuvius would erupt
On Vulcan's feast day, or that a baby's birth

Beneath the fall of a comet might result
In the slaughter of a thousand innocents.
The crows scavenge what they can, are efficient.

The crows, in their crow-like way, do their crow-work,
Tidy up the wreckage, the aftermath.

THE PROBLEM WITH THE FIRST PERSON

I confront silence as if it were a space,
A space altered by my occupying it,
The ragged space, say, of a wilderness.

Each *I* I add to the addendum, to the slippery,
Serpentine *thens* equals, for now, the *now*.
Who am I but fragments and accretions,

A raft built from a shipwreck's scavenged timbers,
A man in the dark as he pulls his shirt over his head,
A malleable metal bent over an anvil's prow

Awaiting the hammer, awaiting the hammer's fall?
Muddled by time, my attention is drawn away
As I aim, as I thumb the arrow's nock, and release.

An angel bends the date palm branch within Joseph's reach.
I am neither the angel nor Joseph but the hunger
One knows intimately and the other can only imagine.

STUDY FOR SALOME DANCING BEFORE HEROD

In the movement toward disappearance,
She is pulled by an undertow of ecstasy.
She wakes in a room where she never fell asleep.
A thousand starlings leaf out a bare tree.
She wakes in a dusky, tenebrous zone.
Evening on the ridges and in the mountains,
But light still spills on the valley floor.
What transport brought her here?
The shape of gravity embodies a pear on the table.
Here time is the only sovereign.
She is like an arrow slipped from its quiver.

CARAVAGGIO'S SEVERED HEADS

The work is hard and messy:
>
> Judith has rolled up her sleeves.

Salome balances the shallow bronze platter
Out from her body so as not to spill.
The boy, David, holds the giant's head at arm's length
Not up high in triumph,
>
> but at a safe distance.

Uncanny the reciprocity of the gaze
— The effects of light arranged to provoke—
When viscous shadows conceal
>
> all not illuminated.

Medusa's curdled blood, it's said, hardens to coral.

It's said the executioner would extort a fee
From the condemned with a promise
To fit the tongue back into the mouth
And close the eyes after death.

MY BROTHER'S INSOMNIA

A boy ties (but will not remember how)
An intricate knot that slips at the slightest tug.

He remembers reading that drops of blood
From Medusa's lopped head bred cobras and asps.

He cares little for snakes, but fears spiders more.
The recluse spider is his least favorite.

Some nights in bed he holds his breath and is dead.
Some nights in bed he holds his breath and listens

To wind rattle the unlocked front door,
To time rustle and scratch in the attic like mice.

He cannot remember if it is summer
Or winter, if sleet or a wren pecks the window.

MY BROTHER'S GHOST

                   I hear him in the hallway,
Short of breath as if his lungs are full of black ore.
He stumbles in his somnambulant shuffling.
He's come back to remind me, but what he says
Is nothing with which my memory coincides.
Don't you remember, he asks? But I do not.
Again he asks, as he must, unselfconscious
About the tedium of his unbidden company.
If he's my brother he's a faded forgery,
Fleshed out as dust motes, an embodied loss
Having missed out, it seems, on the fullness of death.
Perturbed by my refusals and my silence,
He climbs to the attic, sifts through the dross.

TO OPEN THE BODY

The blade eases open the surface:
The edge-shadows crisper
Than the depth's, which are murky,
Estuarial, a flooded foyer.
The unseen wells up into sight.

If from ruins one imagines past grandeur,
One notices in the body the mundane:
Each thing slick, all ooze and welter,
And one begins to doubt a correspondence
Between the animal and the spiritual,

Or, rather, one begins to perceive
No vessel or cranny to hold the soul,
Which certainly must have substance
To counterbalance all that is substantial:
This clutter, this utter realism.

TWO-PART LAMENTATION

As of yet, Jesus is not displaced to a tomb.
A cross holds up the borrowed ladder used to haul him down.
Listen: no seraphic dialogue. Only weeping.
Exhausted, bewildered, bent with suffering,
Figures crowd a shallow space.
Apart from his wounds, Jesus is unmarked,
His body a catenary curve elongating toward the earth.

: :

The artist rigs a coarse rope under its armpits
To hold the cadaver up; its head slumps to its chest,
And where the rope digs in and scores the flesh,
The artists will paint hands to hold and display
A dead Jesus: his punctures, tears, and lashes;
Once such a touch would have drawn out his power,
But today, a cumbersome weight to wield, he is a dead man.

FRAGMENTS FROM AN EXCAVATION

A silver lizard, cast from life, lights the catacombs.

::

As salt attracts dyes and poisons, fog obliterates a grove.

::

Flame-shivers double on dormant waters.

::

To excavate an altar, the sacred is profaned.

::

Look at Mary turn away from the angel, lips still stained.

::

The lead, inert, enacts the semblance of a trance.

::

Buried, one feels the self, and not the stars, move.

::

The borders between elements dissolve.

: :

In vitrines and bell jars: objects commemorate absence.

DARK WAS THE NIGHT

If I blow on a charcoal stick and enliven an ember—
A momentary, lurid light—
                      I might recognize the emptiness
As well as the space I occupy.

                     Moonlight
Or frost:
           gleam of finite deferrals.
How long have I kept the past tarp-covered,

Not on view,
                as if awaiting some final restoration?
The horizon retreats. The distance remains constant,
A dark distance where shadows are quarried.

A dragon of river-mist lifts from the gorge. Moonlight.

The past like a poem, I've come to learn,
Does not change,
                but around it language does.

JUNE DEPRESSION

Once the errant cloud moves on, the sky will heal over.

Today, tomorrow: two sentences hitched by a semicolon.

Although the bees are fire amid blossoms, I carry my depression
    like a bag of ice in winter.

Hemmed in on both sides by ellipses, an hour lasts.

How rare happiness: a white fox born of a snowdrift.

The past? Back there at an impossible distance.

HOME REMEDY

The whiskey made me invisible,
But only to myself.

Back then, one could postpone the future with a story.
The fast creek swirled, gushed, frayed, and entwined,

And a cold wind funneled over its one-lane bridge.
Somewhere the bell note of a fender being bent back to shape:

Tinny, as thin as rain.
Somewhere a river recalled the creek,

Somewhere an ocean its rivers.
I had no story to tell.

The whiskey made me invisible,
A blaze so bright it would silhouette one who stood before it.

A blaze so bright
It would hide one who stood behind it.

To stand in it was to blaze
Effaced.

THE INCREDULITY OF SAINT THOMAS

The locus of pain

Is an opening without coordinates,
A void at the heart of a shrine,

Cloud-blur in the rapids.
At first glance: disorder.

The locus of pain—

An empty space disrupted by time—
Embodies the caesura

Between *gaze* and *gazed upon*,
Threshold and entry.

Enter the wound

As one enters a dream impervious to waking.
Around such silence: turbulence.

One cannot set straight the past
Like a broken bone.

Enter the wound

As if a spirit house,
As if a hallowed precinct.

Forgo the thought
That one alters a space by occupying it.

One does not possess a wilderness.
One enters it.

DEPTH OF FIELD

Fox tracks reveal the past but do not lead to tomorrow.

: :

The mountains wear down to silt,
The silt sifts into dunes.
Things get moved around—

A snowdrift's grammar.

: :

Winter's keen-edged
Scythe-shadow swings
Above stubble.
                    The northern sky,
Bogged down with sleet,
Drags its heavy hull.

: :

How arcane it seems—memory:
Riddled with hermetic gaps,
Its oddly familiar mutable body

A glacier fast on its own melt,
Alive, shape-shifting, gouging out great lakes,
Headlong, erratic. I can hardly remember

Where it began, that it had a beginning,
That I had not always been inching toward
As it inched away.

: :

Once, to my footfall
On an icy wooden bridge
Carp surfaced, expecting to be fed,
Hovered a moment,
Then descended into the murk.

: :

The past is a raveled tapestry,
A furrow cleaved open like scripture.

: :

I am buried alive
In the moment.

A thought arrives
But is avoided, chased away.

Pine wind.
Three thousand visible stars

If I cared to count
The panorama of distinct sparks.

Torn web
Across a broken window.

From the rafters' swallows' nests,
Grit sifts down.

::

The past—imperfect, at a remove—remains.

BENEATH VENUS

Bled through dusk-ore—the evening star.

The roads cross at an oblique angle
The way two narratives dovetail.

Lit by a black and white television
A woman unbraids her hair.

Each night he stops to watch.
He counts the seconds of his gaze

As a boy counts the pages left
In a book he'd like never to end.

As if a charm or heirloom
He carries with him daily his death.

Half a world away bees
Build a hive in a lion carcass.

On the sidewalk home, he hears
A tapping he cannot place—

Perhaps a metronome,
Perhaps chalk on a blackboard

As someone stalls solving for x.

PREPARATORY DRAWING FOR AN UNFINISHED TRIPTYCH

A girl unwinds a skein of yarn as a promise of marriage.

What is a song but a snare with which to capture a moment?

How heavy the bronze quiver, the funerary furniture in the
nocturnal procession from the bride's house to the groom's.

The annunciation is—is it not—a coronation?

To consecrate Eros, they proceed through the doorless aviary
of an orchard, where only an owl roosts.

The painting is *after life*, not *of* the afterlife, *after life* as in *from life*.

As if nude, the bride is the location of *concentrated looking*,
vulnerable to and by being seen. Look at her.

All the world's winds are inventoried in the reedy notes of a panpipe.

In the embalmed moment, they exchange vows and make the
space between them less transient, the nothing therein more
than nothing.

THE TENDED

A mantle of ash mutes the fire,
The source fire they feed
And bank, tend as if a newborn.
A lamp of rendered horse grease,
Its pounded wick of birch bark,
Shadows and reveals a reindeer
Incised on a reindeer shoulder blade.

By dusk a herd fords the meander,
Heads and antlers above water,
Then thunders beyond the alluvial plain
To summer pastures. Unfed, the fire
Would die. So they coax and coo,
Sing to it, offer it straw,
Willow branches, whatever burns.

ARS POETICA

Revealed by a guttering flame, the frieze of horses does not move.

An ice-age later, a stone—its knapped working-edge
That once scraped hides—still fits the palm and is ripe
with function.

Heavier than one might expect. Sharper.

THE ORIGINAL SCRIPTURES NO LONGER EXIST, MERELY TRANSLATIONS OF TRANSLATIONS OF CORRUPTED TEXTS

The torso of God is amber;
Below, fire.

We speak with new tongues,
Take up serpents.

To render (meaning both *replicate* and *reduce*),
God shapes straw-tempered clay.

Beyond the shut gates of Paradise,
A sacrifice of honey and acorns.

The blacksmith feeds the fire
Hazel branches, an effigy of cradled wheat.

The hooded cobra shares a little shade.
What cleft the devil's hoof?

A pruning knife crooked like a crow's beak.

THE IMAGINED SPACE BEYOND

Reliant on memory and fugitive scribbles,

One relinquishes so much
To contingency, to the arbitrary,
To repetitions without understanding,

When what one longs for is artifice.

The quake-fractured fresco
Still functions as a wall to keep separate
The rendered from the imagined space beyond,

The fragmented narrative, patched with dank plaster,

From clouds stalled like thoughts in a darkening sky.
There dusk fuses to the recollection of dusks,

As in an orchard where the fog
Unravels like badly bandaged grafts,
Where shadows of alighting birds

Mark the margin of seeing.

THE DICTATES OF GRAVITY

If one can remember a thing
One never experienced,
Think how easy the forgetting.
At the melting point of lead,
And under ideal conditions,
The spirit transmutes to the material.

::

There, where lucidity blurs,
Ghosts are inherent to half-light:
Construable, if peripheral,
Secrets not yet imparted,
Wind withheld from embers,
Heat mirrored in mirage.

::

The hawk, as if ascending a tower,
Spirals toward the as-of-yet
Legible constellations.
Perspective is a fiction.
Still, one follows parallel lines
To the sharp awl-tip of vanishing.

STILL LIFE

A narrow register of sunlight—
Pearl to smudged silver, dulled by dust,
An octave or so of whites—arranged

As a cluster of stoppered bottles,
Placid, although not inert, not still
As in *stasis,* but still as in *now,*

The still life's objects float as on air
The way the terrace cypresses flame
Up from the cool depth of their shadow.

It is early morning or twilight.
It is the last hour of a siege:
The bottles like a whitewashed city

Shelved above a gorge. Safe. For now.

HERMETICA

A thrown sickle cuts the final sheave.

For a son, bury a stone of black blood.
For a daughter, plait barley, oats, and wheat.

Better the moon's ox-horn crescent than elk
Or bear bones when fashioning a warp-weighted loom.

All things are separated by fire.

The dregs and dross, heavier, settle
While spirits rise, disperse.

To mark swept areas, singe the broom tip.

OBJECTS IN GIORGIO MORANDI'S STUDIO

An absence animates an empty room,
Yet to perceive it, one must enter
And, in entering, displace absence.

The hour (call it *noon sunk in the shallows*)
Is, although it moves on to *isn't*,
As the next and the next and the next hour

Inscribe shadow on water,
Become the shadow of water,
The shadowy, watery light

That is the far wall's marred plaster.
A stack of books on the chair
Must be moved to the stone floor

So that an angel—should an angel enter—
Might have a place to sit down.
Beyond Bologna light pewtered on the sill:

A throb of crickets. Except by dust,
Each bottle, jar, pitcher, vase, tin box, and bowl
Remains untouched, as befits a sacred object.

THE LANGUAGE OF FLOWERS

A broken garland floats on the creek.

Crowfoot, daisy, and rampant widow
Tear free now from a noose of willow.

What does the rosemary remember?

The viola's sorrow? The flattery
Of fennel? The nettle's prick?

The morning chill rough in the meadow
Knows the weedy language of flowers:

The dead men's fingers, the thistle's sting.

Unfaithful, the tall columbine
Hangs its head above the shaded violets.

Who is left to gather the orchids?

The rue that cleansed the afflicted?

PASSAGE

Every few days, I leave a stone on the cairn,
Or sing, out of tune, a line or two

Of Elmore James's "Done Somebody Wrong,"
My mind on the hereafter's sweet waters,

On what words might at last pin down or revoke,
Or moments when lightning simply is. Then isn't.

Everything that happened, you know I am to blame. . . .
I leave a stone to mark my passage, not to account for it.

VENETIAN LIGHT

This morning the light
Changes on the wall opposite:

Hammered-gold, fox-burnt vellum,
A map sun-bleached and blank.
And we call that color *white*.

Last night when you touched my face,

I was like a child whose fever seems a new body,
An amnesiac who recalls he has forgotten,
But not the what.

Detail drained away
As night obscured the buildings' blurred silhouettes,
The facades of mists, the shadowed scaffolds,

The flat water of the canal's curves.

Distant lanterns gleamed, glittered:
A dimly lit world afloat—

A play of horizontals,
Labyrinthine alleys, a fog-bound hour—

A dimly lit world on the verge of submerging.

Diluted by slosh and echoes,
As seen through isinglass
Or a fragile pane of saltwater ice,

Dawn creaked in off the lagoon.

We woke as the light
Changed on the wall opposite.

ESSAY ON IDLENESS

Clear sky,
           but somewhere a shrug of thunder.
The book of noon opens:

Disclosure and redaction on facing pages.

Blue sky like a thrush egg,
Like the underside of a rose leaf.
                        No. The blue of beryl.
No, a drop of breast milk on an infant's cheek,
Flax-flower blue. . . .

Clear sky. A drift of loose spider silk.

Lizard on the serpentine stonewall
Wedges into a crevice.

Somewhere a shrug of thunder.
Somewhere a crow
                (sent by the gods to fetch
The summer rain from sacred springs)

Delays as it waits for a fig to ripen.

THE OTHER SIDE OF THE ARGUMENT

But she prefers the morning glory,
How slowly its bloom unfurls,
How its curl of vine
Catches the flaw in masonry
First, then the crosshatch
Of kite string we hung
From the porch
As a makeshift trellis,
How it needs only a foothold
To fill half the day with blue.

RETURN OF THE EXILE

In order to remember, I have to build
The house brick by remembered brick
Before I can frame in the door, open, enter.

Beneath the flint and steel of stars,
The moon hangs—a butcher's hook.
I sleep in a dim room where

A lampshade is the one thing well-lit.
No bile in my throat.
My heart not yet a bow hard to string,

Not yet a torn nest in a sticker bush.
I am young and can let my soul
Uncoil and slip away like a serpent down an aisle.

I play with matches: some throb,
Some rustle, some are drawn up straight
By a thread of smoke.

Each flame engulfs debris of memory,
Autumnal subtractions, I read as embellishments.

"THE BEAUTIFUL GARDENER" OR
"THE CREATION OF EVE"

I return to the dream as if to a hive
One visits nightly—the air nectar and wax—
Willing to subsist on sweetness. Yet there
Time concentrates like venom, like sunlight
Running as sap high to the branching green.
If I listen I can hear the precise frequency
Friction rubs up that smoky instant before the spark.
Who drew the map I hold, made of shadow-pulp,
Years before I wore down the marked path I follow?
Where am I in the old home movies shot before my birth?
I am not even a ghost haunting the scene,
Not a flare when the frame snags and burns.

REHEARSAL FOR AN ELEGY

Crows roost at dusk, disperse at dawn,
Lumber away as a noisy cortege.
After years of use the millstone is a mirror.

Behind dark chalk hatching,
Behind a shadow-land of pines,
The visible sky glows like blank paper.

If the past were honey
One could scrape it away
With the flat of a knife and be done with sweetness.

THE POPPY

The poppy is a cartouche:
Burnt wadding, sulfur-edged.

Not a scab, but the blood
That wells to form the scab.

Like rhetoric, the purpose
Of the poppy is persuasion,

Yet downcast, with a humor
Too torpid to even muster

What's wrong, the poppy
Is all shrug and crick.

When angels entertained
The holy child, when Eve

Spoke in the serpent's language,
The poppy turned away.

Sawdust and paraffin,
Wheat chaff and clay,

The poppy is Osiris's body,
Spent at last, irredeemable.

PALIMPSEST OF CHALKED EQUATIONS
AND ERASURES

The freight of ambiguity can be figured as
The discrepancy between a and b,
As well as, but different from, a suffuses b.

$::$

Record the last cache of August daylight
As the dark hollow of the plucked raspberry,
As willow-leaf shadow on her nipple.

$::$

That said, each stanza is nonetheless an island,
Joined and separated by the depth and distance
That surrounds, and in surrounding, defines.

$::$

The vacancy marked by the thorn-sharp shriek
Of a redwing blackbird's territorial caw
Is an amalgam of rare and remote elements.

$::$

Record the quicksilver of memory,
All that remains of the past: granaries
Collapsed beneath a bountiful harvest.

FRAGMENT

The past is a point of departure
But from there it is hard to parse the detour or destination.

Even dust is divisible.
Sand transmutes to transparency.

The distance one travels in a day,
What we call a journey, is as far as the space between words,

The distance between sawhorses that hold up a child's casket.
In a dream I am myself but somehow vacant or vacated,

Late, or left behind, unable to fit the little I've brought again into the duffle.
Synonyms, not the words I need, at hand.

Evening river.
A ladder of fire extinguished one rung at a time:

The yellow of buckthorn berry, burry hatchings on gold leaf.
The tense of pain is the present.

Like a deer cornered by a pack of hounds, the *now* freezes.
Something has happened. Something is about to happen.

Although I cannot see beyond it, the window frames an exterior.
What if there were no frame,

No scale, no lens, no vantage point, merely a grid set down?
Although the sound is muted, I can see the actress speaks with a lisp.

Who are these storm-drenched castaways?
Where is this island forged from magma?

I imagine the soundtrack might offer a counterpoint to the
    narrative's murk,
But the commercials come on at such a volume I can't face it.

We all have failures over which to brood.
These acts, ritualized, have lost their savagery and are now symbolic,

And even the antecedents of the symbols have been forgotten.
How does one measure the year: the threshers unpaid? Spring
    floods?

Ice cutters on the river? Ice cluttered on the river?
The car won't start?

What comfort to think that the great beast
Will be thrown into a lake of fire,

That a story, however picaresque, resolves on the final page,
As quaint as that may seem.

Sometimes I feel like one of those castaways—
Shipwrecked, stranded, marooned—

With a single blade, a length of rope, wishing I knew a few more
    poems by heart,
Knew how to start a fire, knew how to spin thread.

That river I mentioned, *evening river* I called it:
No way to map it except to map the history of its meanders.

We know the prophetic in retrospect,
Thus renumber the thousand stars

So that the lines connecting them
Equal *hyena trampled by zebra* or *hero filching fire from the gods.*

Luckily, nothing is impervious to interpretation—
Afterthoughts, premonitions, the slimmest hunches.

This morning, I recalled an old love, fondly, as one should,
Without the what-if. *Recall* is perhaps the wrong word.

Slightly out of focus, between the gaps and lacunae that riddle memory,
I saw her face, or rather a look she'd give me sometimes

That meant to me then *bewildered affection,*
As if already she could imagine her life beyond me.

One rarely recalls the looks on one's own face.
In the mirror all one can do is pose,

Attempt a pose that looks unposed.
Allegories, Walter Benjamin writes, *are in the realm of thought*

What ruins are in the realm of things.
Things, unlike thoughts, are mute, but read as signs,

Shimmer and echo, replete in their articulations,
Or so it seems as the cedar waxwings worry the holly berries
  each year.

In Bruegel's "Procession to Calvary," starlings wheel
Above the crowds that gather at the gallows.

Hard to tell what all the day has in store for them,
Which is the good thief and which the bad.

The windmill perched upon a cliff,
(What could its function be at that height?)

Draws our eyes up to a single storm cloud.
My father would light a cigarette while one still smoked

In the ashtray, gray ash lengthening before it fell.
More often than not he had two or three cigarettes going at once.

I would watch the smoke go from slack and slumped
To thin and taut—an improbable architecture of curlicues,

Tangles and arabesques—as it unraveled itself into nothing.
Hard to pick Jesus out amid that crowd.

A horse skull anchors the painting's lower right corner.
I stand up too quickly, feel dizzy,

Hold onto the library bookshelf until I find my balance.
Or I turn a corner in a hurry and knock

Someone's grocery bag from her hands.
I apologize sincerely and somehow she hears my words,

Hears them and makes sense of them
(that is, it seems, the miracle: that I am a body, not a ghost;

That I make embodied words, not ghost-sounds).
I make small talk as I kneel to pick up a head of cauliflower,

Three limes, and a flat tin of minced clams.
Sometimes I step out into traffic

To hear the tires screech, the horns held.
Hard to recall a time when gravity did not welcome my next step.

Now, as then, sleep leans against the door like a dog waiting to
    be let in.
It is summer. The half-framed-in new construction seems transient:

Parched August straw in a backdraft,
Stick houses passing cars might tumble.

The heat jangles where the road dips,
A mirage darkened with reflection.

Unwilled, the present leaks into the past, tinctures it.
A poem is not a séance and yet how quickly the shades crowd in

Expecting elegy and lamentation.
The moon subtracts zero from zero.

Like an invisible ink one heats to legibility,
The poem reiterates the spent, the long lost, what I tend to call

The nameless haunt of the irremediable,
Yet I go on naming it, nonetheless,

And inter it in words.
I forget just when I started relying on bad memory as an alibi.

AUTUMN DRAWING

The mind is a vertiginous space:
The world beyond it anchored in mere shadow.
One longs for a poetry of flames
But instead hacks and hews,
And like a crying baby, mouth open,
Snatches and grasps at air.

: :

How to render in words a presence
That crosses into absence, the erasures
The pentimenti do not reveal?
As if to explain the ambient light,
A serpentine creek of glacial-melt
Sloughs the quick fire of the auroras.

: :

That rarified luminous matter,
(A surface phenomenon, a blurred tracing,
Like a smolder of sulfur, self-consumed—
Slow, cold, otherworldly—)
As it distills salts from a dream,
Leaves a charged dust on one's tongue.

: :

Hearing a sounded bell tone continue
Into a range of ever-widening waves
One is tempted to express something
About the infinite, but lost in a vibration
At the limit of hearing, one keeps quiet to hear
Into what otherwise might be called *silence*.

BONE FRAGMENTS

Stray frays of virga. Archived in wood grain: graph of annual rainfall.

Thunder, we know, lags back at the speed of sound: the past catches up.

Along the road: barbed wire, telephone poles, vectors and alignments,

A wide array of radio telescopes motionless on rails.

The road—paved, gravel, then dirt—snakes back on itself to move
ahead.

Wind swirls up sand. Sedimentation buries; erosion exhumes.

What have we come to see: a practical field? A modest shrine?

How can one behold and not add to or subtract from the beheld?

Outside Quemado: the ephemeral phenomena of light.

To make art one must make a mark, preserve or disturb the silence.

To define a space, the space beyond it must be surveyed as well.

Imagine a field ringed by, surrounded by, enclosed by mountains.

The subject is not the edge, but the maze inherent within a grid.

No contrails. Today, I've counted nine antelope, eighteen lizards,

Six hares, four jackrabbits, and a falcon perched on a lightning rod.

We talk at the table as the sun goes down, talk on in darkness—

No doubt there are some kinds of knowledge that appear immutable.

This leads some people to think that the stability of contents

Is due to the stability of the container, that the forms

Of rationality are permanent. . . . We talk at the table

As last light flashes, flares, and is extinguished. What is not light seeps in.

Ten thousand stars stand out from the milky smear of the galaxy.

I wake late, find bone fragments you've collected and left on the porch.

I puzzle the pieces: a coyote's ball-and-socket joint,

Or perhaps a gray fox's or a dog's? The cracked femur spills sand.

IF WE NEVER MEET AGAIN THIS SIDE OF HEAVEN

In retrospect,
           even error is essential,
Inevitable,
           if we are to arrive
At what might seem an illogical conjunction:

A fall *or* a cleft. The owl *and* the ax.
A map abstracts,
           thus we find our way.

           : :

Clouds bleed out to blue sky.
The dog scratches at the rug,
           settles in.

Yesterday is a bolus not yet fretted apart.

Tomorrow?
           A tale so enthralling
No one sees the storyteller has levitated.

           : :

The wind, both proof and riddle,
Rustles the stubble,

                spins up chaff.

In the distance, rain falls, yet here nothing

But wind, riddle and proof,
Moonlight

           on the chaff and stubble.

          : :

The soul, forged from ferrous ash,

                     tempered
And hammered to an airy edge, can cut.

If one could pace out one's steps,
Know from the start the end. . .

                no:
If distorts nostalgia, and memory as well.

          : :

I have a heart of flurried snows,
Broken river ice
         like scales, sloughed,
Cold viscous depths,
           dense mercury.

To the end, my heart repeats itself:
Clench and release,
         clench and release, clench. . .

      : :

It's like the shush of a garter snake over pea-gravel,
Or high cloud-wisps wind-frayed to nothing,
This drone,
       this wiry static,
That fills my head when all I want is a word
Or two, the name for this or that
           stark clarity.

      : :

I pawned my chair.

     I pawned my bed.

Ain't got nowhere to lay my head.

Oh lordy me,

     didn't we shake sugaree?

Everything I got is done and pawned.

Everything I got is done and pawned.

    : :

I'll enter the afterlife empty-handed,
Without grave goods or tomb furnishings,
Pockets turned inside out.

      I'll wait for you

Where wisteria overhangs the bank.
You'll recognize my shadow

      by its patches, its frayed cuffs.

    : :

On the banks, a downpour pocks the sand.

Where one might set the horizon,
                              a length
Of string that once mapped a labyrinth,
One finds no edge,
                    only a hung tarp of mottled grays

Behind which entropy has had its way with paradise.

                    : :

An oracle can distill from white noise a tune,
Can read in the flood-tossed rocks the fall of kings,
In blue waxen shadows an infant's fate.

Not me.
              Each day I await a new consonant or vowel,
A new word that might replace
                              the *um*s and *you know*s.

                    : :

Warm wind in the willows rattles like rain,
But no rain for weeks.
                    My mind strays
In every direction like a snake as it moves forward.

Stars appear, Tu Fu writes, *and a thousand doors open.*
Years passed and I failed to open even one.

                    : :

The goatherd whistles and the dog rounds up
The stragglers.
                    Here, an eon ago one might have heard
A song played on a flute fashioned from a goat's shinbone.
Two notes like the goatherd's whistle—
                              hardly a song—
Still song enough to imagine a third, a fourth, and a fifth.

                    : :

I am practicing detachment,
                 and have become artful
At the practice, but not the detachment.

Bored, I notice that I am hungry;
Hungry, that I am bored with what's in the fridge.

I am a rich man trying to enter heaven.

       : :

Time to stop musing
             and get to work.

Cold sunlight chimes on tide-exposed rocks.
Frost flowers on marsh heather.
Wind buffets the gull's scraggly cry.

The conundrum:
          musing *is* my work.

   : :

Depression, as you know,

                        is all brambles and weeds,

Is an alloy of lead and slumber,

                          a spent ember

That magnifies the dark and depth beneath an iced surface.

Sometimes you break through for a breath

Before anger's rusted anchor drags you back down.

        : :

Snow-dust, a momentary ghost spun up,

                               disperses.

Ice binds up creeks and streams.

At the heart of winter's maze, refuge.

How much heat to render the mind?

All day I gather deadfall for the fire.

        : :

A narrow spectrum reveals the little I see.

Where the path steepens,
                              a spotted fawn startles,
But the dog could care less,
                              nose down,
Busy making sense of history.

Camouflaged in the dapple, the fawn disappears.

                    : :

The shaved crystals of cicada wings
Refract summer light from thirty years ago.

You pour another glass
                              as cicadas whirr in the pines.

We Poets, you offer as a toast,
                              in our youth begin in gladness;
But thereof come in the end despondency and madness.

                    : :

The garden, it turns out, is an offering
To the deer, squirrels, and foxes.

They leave behind hoof and paw prints,
Torn vines and broken stalks,

                        some shit to season the soil.

Today there's rain, so no need to water.

        : :

And the fools replied,
                Lord, when was it that we saw you hungry
And gave you food
            or thirsty and gave you something to drink?
And when was it that we saw you a stranger
                    and welcomed you,
Or naked and gave you clothing?
And when was it that we saw you sick
              or in prison and visited you?

        : :

A book falls from my hand and wakes me.

Midday
      yet in a dream, my friend, you're driving
Your red Fiat down Providence Road at night—
Wipers can't keep up with the rain—
And through a hole in the floorboard,

                        I watch the earth spin by.

      ::

The realm of God is likened to the smallest mustard seed,
That when sown grows into a tree—
                        its branches reach the sky—
And the birds of the air dwell in its shade.

A grieving woman is sent to fetch a mustard seed,
A mustard seed from a house where no one has known grief.

      ::

In a poem of leave-taking,

                 one friend bids farewell

To the other, who follows a path

That follows a stream that has no spring.

The spring is dry, but not the stream,

Not yet at this point in the journey.

              : :

Vast stars across the depths.

The moon,

                faceless, thumb-worn,

Is as empty as my mind tonight,

Reflective, but dully, coldly

Whole until its edges wear away.

              : :

A rain-drenched fox crosses the graveyard
But does not take cover
                      beneath a tent
That shelters a just-dug grave.

Bedraggled, skinnier than one would imagine,
The fox stops once to look up at the rain
                            then lopes away.

           : :

Before the wine wore off,
                  we stood on the levee at dawn,
Watched the rivers converge.

I broke a stick and threw the two ends
Haphazardly and roused
                a cottonmouth that hid amid dead leaves.

From the levee, we watched the rivers converge.

NOTES

ASH: after Zhang Huan.

SPIRIT FIGURES: section seven borrows from Wang Wei.

JUNE DEPRESSION: is dedicated to Michael Friedman; the third line owes a nod to Michael Friedman's song "Don't Let the Bastards Get You Down" from his album *Cool of the Coming Dark*.

TWO-PART LAMENTATION: part one after Rogier van der Weyden.

FRAGMENTS FROM AN EXCAVATION: is dedicated to H. L. Hix; after Thomas Lyon Mills.

THE INCREDULITY OF SAINT THOMAS: after Anish Kapoor.

STILL LIFE: after Giorgio Morandi.

ESSAY ON IDLENESS: after James Turrell.

"THE BEAUTIFUL GARDENER" OR "THE CREATION OF EVE": after Max Ernst.

BONE FRAGMENTS: after Walter De Maria; the italicized passage is Gaston Bachelard.

IF WE NEVER MEET AGAIN THIS SIDE OF HEAVEN: is dedicated to José del Valle; section seven quotes from Elizabeth Cotton's song "Shake Sugaree"

ACKNOWLEDGMENTS

The author offers many thanks to the editors of the following periodicals where many of these poems, often in earlier versions, first found readers:

Art and Academe:
BENEATH VENUS
THE PROBLEM WITH THE FIRST PERSON
Basilica Review:
RETURN OF THE EXILE
Beloit Poetry Journal:
DARK WAS THE NIGHT
PALIMPSEST OF CHALKED EQUATIONS AND ERASURES
Denver Quarterly:
THE ORIGINAL SCRIPTURES NO LONGER EXIST, MERELY
TRANLATIONS OF TRANSLATIONS OF CORRUPTED TEXTS
Drunken Boat:
DICTATES OF GRAVITY
IF WE NEVER MEET AGAIN THIS SIDE OF HEAVEN
Field:
MY BOTHER'S INSOMNIA
The Gettysburg Review:
VENETIAN LIGHT
WORKING IN THE DARK
Grand Street:
THE OTHER SIDE OF THE ARGUMENT
Interdisciplinary Literary Studies:
PASSAGE
SPIRIT FIGURES

The Kenyon Review:

ASH

PREPARATORY DRAWING FOR AN UNFINISHED TRIPTYCH

New World Writing:

AUTUMN DRAWING

Nimrod:

ESSAY ON IDLENESS

JUNE DEPRESSION

Literature and Belief:

THE POPPY

Plume:

FRAGMENT

Poetry:

THE LANGUAGE OF FLOWERS

Poets.org:

STUDY FOR SALOME DANCING BEFORE HEROD

In Quire:

FRAGMENTS FROM AN EXCAVATION

The Southwest Review:

OBJECTS IN GIORGIO MORANDI'S STUDIO

Spirituality and Health:

THE BOOK OF AN HOUR

St. Katherine Review:

REHEARSAL FOR AN ELEGY

Talking River:

DEPTH OF FIELD

WHEN WE MEET ON THAT BEAUTIFUL SHORE

Web Conjunctions:

BONE FRAGMENTS

Eric Pankey is the author of eleven books of poetry. His poetry, essays, and reviews have appeared widely in such journals as *The Iowa Review*, *The New Yorker*, and *The Kenyon Review*. He is a professor of English and the Heritage Chair in Writing at George Mason University. He currently resides in Fairfax, VA.

Interior design & typesetting by Mary Austin Speaker

Typeset in Granjon

Modeled after Claude Garamond's roman typeface, Granjon was
designed by George W. Jones for Linotype & Machinery in 1928.